LINDSAY

PICK ME UP

- SOMETHING TO CHEER YOU UP

- A SELF-AWARE CRY FOR ATTENTION

- LITERALLY HOW TO USE THIS BOOK (OPEN AT RANDOM)

LINDSAY

Adam

PICK ME UP

A PEP TALK FOR NOW & LATER

ADAM J. KURTZ

(AUTHOR OF 1 Page AT A TIME)

A TARCHERPERIGEE BOOK

An imprint of Penguin Random House LLC
375 Hudson Street
New York, New York 10014

COPYRIGHT © 2016 BY ADAM J. KURTZ

Tarcher and Perigee are registered trademarks, and the
colophon is a trademark of Penguin Random House LLC.

Most TarcherPerigee books are available at special quantity
discounts for bulk purchase for sales promotions, premiums,
fund-raising, and educational needs. Special books or book
excerpts also can be created to fit specific needs. For details,
write: SpecialMarkets@penguinrandomhouse.com.

ISBN 9780143109082

Printed in the United States of America
3 5 7 9 10 8 6 4

DEDICATED TO
THE FUTURE

& IN LOVING
MEMORY OF

THE PAST

BUT THAT'S
NEVER REALLY
STOPPED ME
BEFORE

START (SOMEWHERE)

THIS BOOK IS ALL ABOUT WHO YOU ARE & WHAT YOU KNOW.

PICK IT UP ANY TIME YOU NEED SOME DISTRACTION OR ENCOURAGEMENT.

OPEN TO ANY PAGE NOW & LEAVE YOUR MARK FOR LATER. WRITE WITH A CLEAR MIND THEN RETURN WHEN YOU NEED SOME OF YOUR OWN ADVICE, OR A REMINDER OF JUST HOW MUCH YOU'RE CAPABLE OF.

→

FIND YOUR WAY BACK
THROUGH THIS JOURNEY
WITH A PAPER TRAIL
ON THE INTERNET.
POST WITH #PICKMEUPBOOK
SO YOU CAN SEARCH LATER.

THE ONLY THING
THAT
ACTUALLY
ACTUALLY

MATTERS

IS BEING HAPPY
WITH WHAT
YOU'VE GOT &
LEARNING TO
MAKE THE
BEST OF IT.

DESCRIBE YOUR MOOD
IN 1 WORD EVERY TIME
YOU VISIT THIS PAGE:

_____   _____

_____   _____

_____   _____

_____   _____

_____   _____

_____   _____

_____   _____

DEATH IS INEVITABLE SO SHUT UP & ENJOY YOUR TIME
ACCEPT
DECLINE

WHO DO YOU ADMIRE & WHY?
DRAW A PORTRAIT & TAG THEM!

WHY ARE YOU SO
PETRIFIED OF SILENCE?
HERE, CAN YOU HANDLE THIS:

WRITE SOME
GOOD ADVICE

THEN TAKE IT!

ADMIT IT:

FEELING SORRY FOR MYSELF

ADMIT ONE

V.I.P. ACCESS

ANXIOUS FOR NO REASON

ADMIT 1

LIMITED ENGAGE-MENT

STAYING IN & ORDERING A PIZZA

ADMIT ONE

1 NIGHT ONLY

DRAW SOME
AWARDS NOW,
THEN GIVE THEM
TO YOURSELF
LATER!

EVERYONE HAS VICES.
WE KNOW THEY CAN
BE BAD FOR US, LIKE
CANDY OR BEER, BUT
WE INDULGE ANYWAY.
HELP YOURSELF BY
MAKING THEM TREATS
& NOT THE EXPECTATION.

DESCRIBE THINGS
YOU CAN FEEL

BUT NOT EASILY SEE

IT'S OKAY &
PROBABLY HEALTHY
TO BE "AN OPEN BOOK,"
BUT HANDLE YOURSELF
WITH CARE.

BE GENTLE OR YOU'LL
LOSE YOUR PLACE,
OR WORSE,
CRACK YOUR SPINE.

ADVICE YOU GAVE RECENTLY THAT YOU MIGHT NEED YOURSELF:

_____

_____

_____

_____

_____

_____

_____

DRAW A BATH ANY
TIME YOU NEED TO
CHILL

ADD BANDAGES TO THIS PAGE
SO IT DOESN'T FALL APART

IT CAN BE
SCARY OR HARD
TO BE TRUE TO
YOURSELF.

YOU MAY NEED
TO BIDE YOUR
TIME UNTIL THE
RIGHT MOMENT.

BUT YOU ONLY
GET ONE LIFE

& YOU DESERVE
TO LIVE IT

FOR REAL.

APOLOGIZE TO YOURSELF

- SORRY I DIDN'T TRUST YOU
- SORRY I STAYED UP SO LATE

IT'S A BIRTHDAY! THE WORLD IS FULL OF PEOPLE CELEBRATING EVERY DAY.

DRAW AN EXTRA CANDLE EACH TIME YOU'RE HERE, THEN BLOW THEM ALL OUT WHEN YOUR BIRTHDAY COMES.

REPEAT AFTER ME:

IF I CAN'T BE "AMAZING,"
I'LL BE "~~FUCK~~ING AMAZING"
INSTEAD.

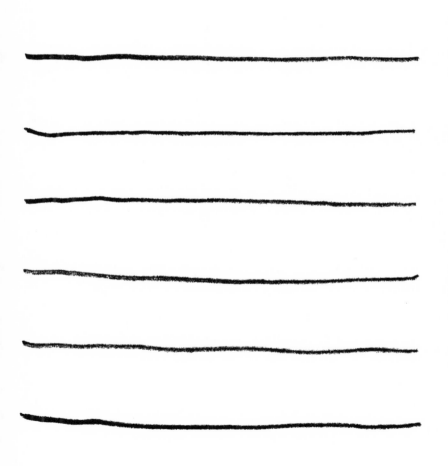

DRAW YOUR LAST MEAL:

NOW

LATER

AGAIN

SOON

DESSERT

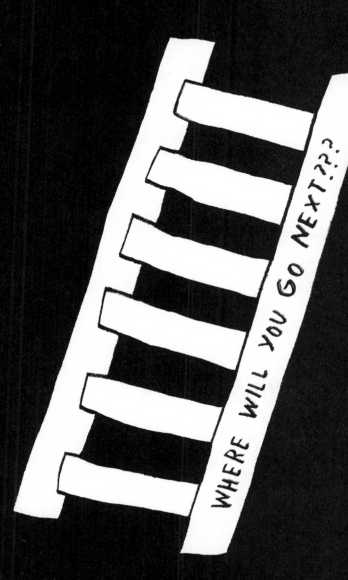

THE WORLD IS
BIG & I AM NOT
BUT I AM STILL
ENOUGH

FIND A BONE TO PICK THEN <u>BURY</u> IT!

I'M ANGRY ABOUT:

I'M ANNOYED BY:

WORRIED FOR:

MAD AT:

I CAN'T STAND:

WISH I COULD FORGET:

POST & TAG YOUR BFF
#PICKMEUPBOOK

WHAT CAN YOU BUILD
WITH A SMALL STEP NOW?

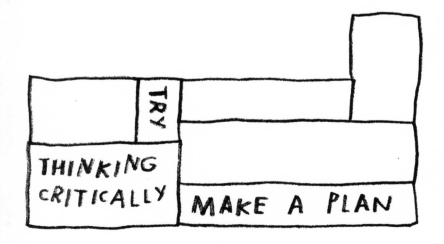

EVERYONE HAS TO GO
SOMEDAY SO WE JUST
HAVE TO ENJOY THE
JOURNEY. BE A GOOD
PERSON, MAKE
POSITIVE CHANGE,
& MAYBE HAVE
A COOKIE.

TTYL

ULTIMATE BUCKET LIST

FILL THE LIST WITH YOUR DREAM ACTIVITIES OR
ACHIEVEMENTS, THEN PUT IT INTO THE WORLD

1 _____

2 _____

3 _____

4 _____

5 _____

6 _____

7 _____

8 _____

9 _____

10 _____

DRAW A SLICE OF BREAD.
DRAW A TOASTER.
COME BACK SOON OR
YOU'RE BURNT TOAST!

HELLO?

HI?

SORRY,

YOU'RE

BREAKING

UP!

TEAR & CRUMPLE THIS
PAGE BIT BY BIT

IT'S A VERY STRANGE TIME
TO BE ALIVE, WHEN WE
CAN SHARE PRIVATE IDEAS
& FEELINGS INSTANTLY,
ON THE INTERNET.

REMEMBER THAT LIKES,
NOTES, FAVES & SHARES
ARE JUST NUMBERS &
DON'T LET THAT GET TO
YOU. SURE, WE ALL LIKE
TO BE HEARD, BUT WHEN
EVERYONE'S SHOUTING
AT ONCE, IT ALL SORT OF
GETS A BIT LOST.

DID YOU KNOW:

- HARD WORK CAN PAY OFF
- LOVE IS ACTUALLY REAL
- DEATH IS INEVITABLE

TAKE A DEEP BREATH.
HOLD FOR THREE SECONDS,
THEN EXHALE BELOW:

TAKE A CHILL PILL.
DRAW SOME TO TAKE LATER.

IF OUR EYES ARE THE
WINDOWS TO THE SOUL,
MAKE SURE TO READ
ANY POSTED SIGNS.

HELP
WANTED
———————
INQUIRE
WITHIN

HELP
YOUR
SELF

PLEASE NOTE:

WATCH
YOUR
STEP!

WRITE SOMETHING TO WORK ON
OR GROW THROUGH RIGHT NOW:

NOW _____

LATER _____

NEXT TIME _____

AGAIN _____

SOON _____

SOMETIME _____

ONCE MORE _____

I AM TRYING
VERY HARD TO
DISAPPEAR
RIGHT NOW,
PLEASE GO TO
ANOTHER
PAGE

CELEBRATE EVERYTHING!

WHAT CAN YOU CELEBRATE TODAY?

KEEP CLIMBING ON & UP
(MAYBE ADD A HANDRAIL)

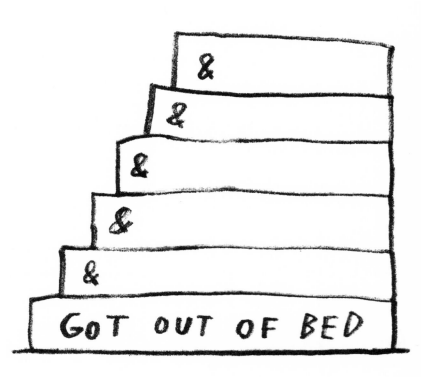

WHAT'S A RECENT ACCOMPLISHMENT YOU NEVER THOUGHT WAS POSSIBLE?

NOW _____

LATER _____

NEXT TIME _____

AGAIN _____

SOON _____

SOMETIME _____

ONCE MORE _____

THERE'S SOMETHING SPECIAL
ABOUT BEING ALONE IN ANOTHER
PLACE. IF YOU'VE BEEN FEELING
A LITTLE WEIRD, MAYBE GIVE
YOURSELF TIME FOR A SOLO
JOURNEY. NONE OF THAT
 "EAT PRAY LOVE" STUFF,
JUST TIME TO REMEMBER
 YOUR BASIC INSTINCTS.

OKAY, MAYBE YOU
SHOULD EAT SOMETHING
THOUGH.

ADD A COMMENT WITH
EACH VISIT, THEN TRY TO
NEVER READ THEM AGAIN!

DRAW COFFEE CUPS,
EACH SHAKIER THAN
THE LAST:

EMOTIONS AREN'T
ALWAYS RATIONAL
SO JUST WRITE THEM
DOWN & DON'T WORRY
ABOUT EXPLAINING
THEM RIGHT NOW.

WHAT COULD GO WRONG:

WHAT ACTUALLY HAPPENED:

CONNECT THE DOGS:

AHH! SORRY, I MEANT DOTS!
F~~UCKING~~ AUTOCORRECT!!

EMOTIONAL BREAKDOWN

HOW DO YOU FEEL?

[ ]

WHY?

[ ]

HOW LONG?

[ ]

WHO KNOWS?

[ ]

WILL THIS LAST?

(YES)

(NO)

HOW WILL YOU
HANDLE IT?

FORGET
ABOUT IT!

[ ]

TODAY'S DATE: _____

ENJOY THE
UNKNOWN

WHILE YOU
STILL CAN

SMART ~~ASS~~

CURRENT BEST FRIEND:

DATE _____ FRIEND _____

DATE _____ FRIEND _____

DATE _____ FRIEND _____

DATE _____ FRIEND _____

DATE _____ FRIEND _____

DATE _____ FRIEND _____

DATE _____ FRIEND _____

DATE _____ FRIEND _____

DATE _____ FRIEND _____

DATE _____ FRIEND _____

COUNT YOUR BLESSINGS
& WATCH THEM PILE UP

MAYBE YOU'RE
NOT AS ALONE
AS YOU THOUGHT

THE INTERNET
IS DETACHED,
BUT PEOPLE
ARE REAL

WE ARE ALL
CONNECTED

SHARE ANY TIME
#PICKMEUPBOOK

HAVE YOU EVER HAD YOUR HEART BROKEN?
IT'S REALLY JUST PROOF THAT LOVE IS
REAL, AND OUT THERE! OF COURSE THERE
WILL BE PLENTY MORE TO COME.

IF IT'S BEEN A WHILE, YOU MIGHT BE
STARTING TO FORGET. HOLD ON TO
THOSE MOMENTS WHEN LOVE WAS
UNDENIABLE, EVEN IF THEY'RE KIND
OF BITTERSWEET NOW.

TIME IS LIKE A THREAD. A STITCH IS
NOT VERY STRONG, BUT MANY STITCHES
CAN MEND ANYTHING. SEW OR DRAW A
NEW STITCH NOW & ADD MORE LATER.

WHAT'S YOUR (CURRENT) GREATEST CHALLENGE?

NOW _____

LATER _____

NEXT TIME _____

AGAIN _____

SOON _____

SOMETIME _____

ONCE MORE _____

DRAW A STRAW IN A
TOUGH SITUATION &
SUCK IT UP!

WRITE THANK-YOU NOTES TO YOURSELF

THANK YOU FOR

I APPRECIATE

MAN, YOU REALLY

THANKS AGAIN

IT MEANT A LOT WHEN

A TOKEN OF MY GRATITUDE

OKAY, THANKS, LOVE YOU!!

QUICK, COVER YOUR SCREEN
BEFORE YOUR BOSS SEES!

DRAW YOUR
  CURRENT SELF:

NOW

LATER

AGAIN

SOON

HOW (NOT) TO LIVE A FULFILLING LIFE

- COMPARE YOURSELF TO OTHERS REGULARLY

- OBSESS ABOUT ALL THE THINGS THAT CAN GO WRONG

- QUESTION THE MOTIVES OF THOSE WHO LOVE YOU & PUSH THEM AWAY

- NEVER PLAN AHEAD

- IGNORE YOUR BODY & MIND WHEN THEY GIVE YOU WARNING SIGNS

- EXPECT EVERYTHING WHILE GIVING NOTHING

THE FIRST THOUGHT YOU HAD TODAY:

NOW _____

LATER _____

NEXT TIME _____

AGAIN _____

SOON _____

SOMETIME _____

ONCE MORE _____

CROSS OUT SOME NEGATIVITY ANY TIME YOU'RE HERE

NEGATIVITY   NEGATIVITY   NEGATIVITY
NEGATIVITY   NEGATIVITY   NEGATIVITY
NEGATIVITY   NEGATIVITY   NEGATIVITY
NEGATIVITY   NEGATIVITY   NEGATIVITY
NEGATIVITY   NEGATIVITY   NEGATIVITY
NEGATIVITY   NEGATIVITY   NEGATIVITY
NEGATIVITY   NEGATIVITY   NEGATIVITY
NEGATIVITY   NEGATIVITY   NEGATIVITY
NEGATIVITY   NEGATIVITY   NEGATIVITY
NEGATIVITY   NEGATIVITY   NEGATIVITY
NEGATIVITY   NEGATIVITY   NEGATIVITY
NEGATIVITY   NEGATIVITY   NEGATIVITY
NEGATIVITY   NEGATIVITY   NEGATIVITY
NEGATIVITY   NEGATIVITY   NEGATIVITY
NEGATIVITY   NEGATIVITY   NEGATIVITY
NEGATIVITY   NEGATIVITY   NEGATIVITY

DRAW THE DEEP END,
THEN DIVE RIGHT IN.

EVERYONE LEAVES
   EVENTUALLY.
DRAW MORE & WATCH
YOUR FOREST GROW.

DESCRIBE LAST NIGHT'S DREAM IN 3 WORDS:

_____ _____ _____

_____ _____ _____

_____ _____ _____

_____ _____ _____

_____ _____ _____

_____ _____ _____

_____ _____ _____

_____ _____ _____

_____ _____ _____

YOU'VE BEEN SENT
A RAY OF SUNSHINE!

FORWARD THIS PAGE
TO FIVE PEOPLE NOW
& ALL YOUR DAYS WILL
BE FULL OF LOVE & LIGHT.

IF YOU IGNORE THIS,
BE WARNED, LITERALLY
NOTHING WILL HAPPEN-
BUT YOU'RE NOT A VERY
THOUGHTFUL FRIEND,
ARE YOU??

WHERE TO NEXT?

"IMPOSSIBLE"
CHALLENGES

MEMORIES

FOUNDATION

DRAW YOURSELF AS MUCH
EXTRA HELP AS YOU NEED:

OF COURSE FAILURE IS AN OPTION
DON'T BE RIDICULOUS IT'S LIKE
ONE OF TWO MAIN OPTIONS
& ALSO IT'S GONNA BE FINE.

"HOME" CAN BE A PLACE,
A PERSON, OR SOMETHING ELSE.
WHAT FEELS LIKE HOME NOW?

NOW _____

LATER _____

NEXT TIME _____

AGAIN _____

SOON _____

SOMETIME _____

ONCE MORE _____

DRAW YOUR FAVORITE BOOK:

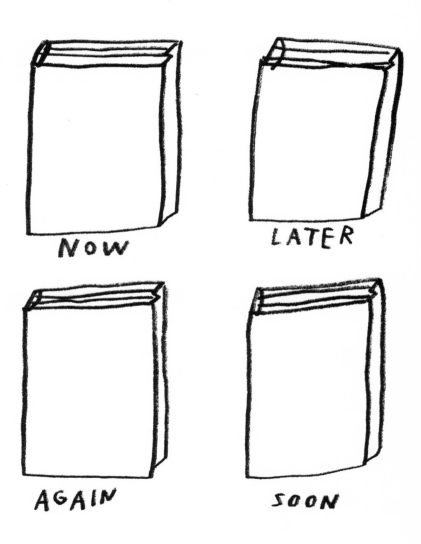

NOW

LATER

AGAIN

SOON

DISAPPEAR (FROM THE INTERNET)
FOR A DAY. SHARE HERE INSTEAD
& POST THIS PAGE LATER.

EVERYTHING

YOU

ELSE

WRITE A SECRET
ENCOURAGEMENT
FOR THE FUTURE.
DON'T SHARE THIS!

HOW DO YOU FEEL TODAY?

DO NOT
DISTURB:

ANY TIME
YOU ARRIVE
AT THIS PAGE,
CLOSE THE BOOK.

SIT QUIETLY
FOR A MINUTE.

SOMETIMES YOU
JUST HAVE TO WAIT.

INSECURITY
IS LIKE A PRECIOUS
TREASURE
TO INSPIRE &
MOTIVATE, SO BURY
THAT ~~SHIT~~ DEEP
& DON'T TELL
EVERYONE
ABOUT IT.

THINK ABOUT EVERYTHING THAT
YOU DIDN'T KNOW YOU COULD DO,
UNTIL YOU DID IT ANYWAY.

START A LIST & ADD AS YOU RETURN.

_____   _____

_____   _____

_____   _____

_____   _____

_____   _____

_____   _____

_____   _____

_____   _____

_____   _____

_____   _____

POST THIS ANY TIME
YOU LITERALLY CANNOT

📷 #PICKMEUPBOOK

WHAT'S SOMETHING YOU CAN IMPROVE ON??

NOW _____

LATER _____

NEXT TIME _____

AGAIN _____

SOON _____

SOMETIME _____

ONCE MORE _____

YOUR TRUE MOTIVATION
MAY BE INTANGIBLE,
BUT MAYBE SEEING
THIS PAGE FROM TIME
TO TIME WILL BE A
USEFUL REMINDER
TO STAY FOCUSED ON
YOUR GOALS & DREAMS.

CHECK SOMETHING OFF YOUR LIST:

☐ ☐ ☐ ☐ ☐ ☐ ☐ ☐ ☐ ☐
☐ ☐ ☐ ☐ ☐ ☐ ☐ ☐ ☐ ☐
☐ ☐ ☐ ☐ ☐ ☐ ☐ ☐ ☐ ☐
☐ ☐ ☐ ☐ ☐ ☐ ☐ ☐ ☐ ☐
☐ ☐ ☐ ☐ ☐ ☐ ☐ ☐ ☐ ☐
☐ ☐ ☐ ☐ ☐ ☐ ☐ ☐ ☐ ☐
☐ ☐ ☐ ☐ ☐ ☐ ☐ ☐ ☐ ☐
☐ ☐ ☐ ☐ ☐ ☐ ☐ ☐ ☐ ☐
☐ ☐ ☐ ☐ ☐ ☐ ☐ ☐ ☐ ☐
☐ ☐ ☐ ☐ ☐ ☐ ☐ ☐ ☐ ☐
☐ ☐ ☐ ☐ ☐ ☐ ☐ ☐ ☐ ☐
☐ ☐ ☐ ☐ ☐ ☐ ☐ ☐ ☐ ☐
☐ ☐ ☐ ☐ ☐ ☐ ☐ ☐ ☐ ☐
☐ ☐ ☐ ☐ ☐ ☐ ☐ ☐ ☐ ☐

IT'S SO SATISFYING!

A BLANK PAGE CAN BE
TERRIFYING, SO FILL THIS
PAGE IN BIT BY BIT
WHENEVER YOU'RE HERE.

I KNOW
YOU
SLEEP
BUT LIKE,
DO YOU
EVEN
DREAM,

BRO??

OKAY, WHAT'S YOUR EXCUSE THIS TIME??

NOW _____

LATER _____

NEXT TIME _____

AGAIN _____

SOON _____

SOMETIME _____

ONCE MORE _____

PUT A TINY VOICE
IN EACH HEAD:

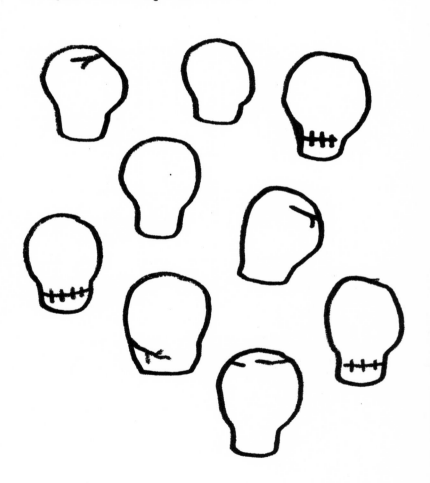

DRAW SOMETHING GREAT SO
YOU CAN COME BACK &
BE ALL PROUD OR WHATEVER

I'M DEAD

YOU'RE NOT
(CHEER UP)

WHAT ARE YOU AFRAID OF?
WRITE ONE THING NOW, THEN
FACE IT NEXT TIME & ADD ANOTHER!

_____

_____

(OKAY NOW FACE IT)

_____

_____

(STARE IT DOWN)

_____

_____

(DEAL WITH IT)

_____

_____

(YOU GOT THIS)

_____

_____

(WHAT FEAR? YOU'RE INVINCIBLE!!!)

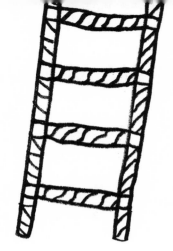

EMERGENCY
EXIT
_____
LET'S GET OUT
OF HERE!

DRAW A MAP OF YOUR FRIEND'S HOUSE.
MARK THEM WITH AN "X" SO YOU
CAN TREASURE THEM FOREVER.

KNOW YOUR WORTH
KNOW YOUR VALUE

STOP TRYING TO IMPRESS
OR CONVINCE SOMEONE
WHO DOESN'T CARE.
FOCUS ON THE PEOPLE WHO
ARE WILLING, ABLE &
RECEPTIVE. YOU CAN'T
WASTE TIME ON SOMEONE
WHO DOESN'T LOVE OR
RESPECT YOU. DO YOUR
THING & LET THE REST
HAPPEN (OR NOT).

COME BACK ANY TIME YOU
NEED TO READ THIS AGAIN.

WRITE YOUR UNPOPULAR OPINIONS, THEN KEEP THEM TO YOURSELF!

- FRENCH FRIES ARE GROSS
- I HATE TO RELAX

PLANT YOUR GARDEN:

EMOTION BINGO

LOVE	DIS- APPOINT MENT	ABLE	CALM	LOVED
ENJOY- MENT	ANXIOUS	WORRY	ANGER	WONDER
APPRE- CIATION	GREAT	FREE SPACE	CONTENT	BRAVE
SATIS- FIED	TRUST	FEAR	FRUST- RATION	REST- LESS
CURIOUS	EXCITE- MENT	PEACE	ENCOU- RAGED	JOY

MARK A CURRENT FEELING
ANY TIME YOU'RE ON THIS PAGE.
FIVE IN A ROW WINS!

LIFE IS UNPREDICTABLE
BUT PATTERNS FORM

GOALS FOR THIS YEAR

_____

_____

_____

_____

_____

_____

_____

_____

_____

_____

_____

_____

_____

ERROR 404:

THE PAGE COULD
NOT BE DISPLAYED

DRAW A NEW DOOR EACH TIME
So YOU CAN GET
OUT OF HERE!

EXIT

OKAY, SO LIKE,
WHAT DOES
"LIVE LIKE YOU'RE DYING"
EVEN MEAN?

OF COURSE YOU'RE DYING,
WE ALL ARE, BUT
PROBABLY NOT TOMORROW
SO WHY SPEND TODAY
"LIVING" FRANTICALLY?

THERE IS SO MUCH TO BE
GRATEFUL FOR!
WRITE ONE THING NOW &
ADD MORE LATER.

_____   _____

_____   _____

_____   _____

_____   _____

_____   _____

_____   _____

_____   _____

_____   _____

_____   _____

_____   _____

HEY! HERE'S AN IDEA:
MAYBE TRY TO
LOWER YOUR
EXPECTATIONS &
ENJOY WHAT YOU
HAVE??

DRAW SOMETHING UNREMARKABLE.
NEXT TIME GIVE IT SOME MAGIC!

EMOTIONAL BREAKDOWN

HOW DO YOU FEEL?

WHY?

HOW LONG?

WHO KNOWS?

WILL THIS LAST?

YES

NO

HOW WILL YOU HANDLE IT?

FORGET ABOUT IT!

TODAY'S DATE: _____

FIND YOUR WAY
THROUGH THE DARK

OKAY

TAPE A $5 BILL
TO THIS PAGE TO
SPEND ON YOUR
    FIFTH VISIT HERE

TREAT COUNTDOWN:

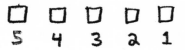

5   4   3   2   1

FEELING BAD?
THERE'S AN APP FOR THAT!

WHAT'S SOMETHING STUPID
YOU'VE CAUGHT YOURSELF
DOING RECENTLY?

NOW _____

LATER _____

NEXT TIME _____

AGAIN _____

SOON _____

SOMETIME _____

ONCE MORE _____

LET YOUR MIND CLEAR FULLY.
FOCUS ONLY ON YOUR
BREATHING & FLOAT AWAY
FOR A WHILE. WHEN YOU
COME BACK HERE, YOU'LL
KNOW WHAT TO DO.

DRAW GOOD-LUCK CHARMS,
THEN CUT THEM OUT AS NEEDED:

THINGS I CAN FOCUS ON

- STAYING POSITIVE
- TANGIBLE ACCOMPLISHMENTS
- SELECT INTANGIBLE ACCOMPLISHMENTS
- BEING A DECENT PERSON

THINGS I CAN NOT FOCUS ON

- NEGATIVITY
- SELF-DOUBT
- THINGS BEYOND MY CONTROL
- ANY OF YOUR BULL~~SHIT~~

MEET YOUR MATCH:

IT'S NOT BIG, EXPENSIVE OR MODERN, BUT IT CAN CREATE GREAT CHANGE FOR BETTER OR WORSE.

IT'S NOT UNIQUE, BUT RATHER ONE OF MANY, AND YET IF USED WELL, THIS ONE MIGHT BURN THE LONGEST & BRIGHTEST OF ALL.

WHENEVER YOU'RE HERE
FIND A DARK PLACE
TO COLLECT YOUR THOUGHTS,
THEN WRITE ONE DOWN:

INCREASE YOUR
ENGAGEMENT BY
AFFIXING TO
YOUR BUTT:

#PICKMEUPBOOK

DRAW YOUR GUTS, THEN
TRY TO TRUST THEM.

I DON'T
KNOW WHY
THIS EXISTS
BUT I'M
GLAD IT DOES.

THERE'S A FINE LINE
BETWEEN JEALOUSY &
INSPIRATION. HOW CAN
YOU GROW FROM THIS
FEELING?

WRITE A TINY WISH
THEN GLUE IT FACEDOWN
ON THE PAGE. KEEP ON
MAKING WISHES!

DRAW YOURSELF NOW

SEEMINGLY IMPOSSIBLE CHALLENGE

THEN DO IT AGAIN LATER

A WORD
YOU'VE NEVER TRULY UNDERSTOOD BEFORE:

_____   _____

_____   _____

_____   _____

_____   _____

_____   _____

_____   _____

_____   _____

_____   _____

_____   _____

_____   _____

ONE "YES" LEADS TO ANOTHER!
ADD MORE WHEN YOU'RE HERE.

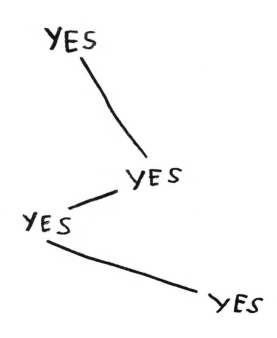

YOU CAN BE YOUR OWN SUPPORT SYSTEM

CARRY YOURSELF WITH DIGNITY & COMPASSION

& REMEMBER TO LIFT WITH YOUR LEGS, NOT YOUR BACK

TEAR A SMALL PIECE OF THIS
PAGE TO CARRY WITH YOU.
TAKE A LITTLE MORE NEXT
TIME TOO. ENJOY FEELING
CONNECTED TO THE REST OF
YOUR THOUGHTS IN THIS BOOK.

DRAW YOUR BODY &
LABEL YOUR INNER STRENGTHS:

YOU CAN GO FORWARD
BUT NOT BACK
BECAUSE LIFE MOVES ON
WHETHER YOU'RE READY
OR NOT

DON'T BE AFRAID
TO SPEAK UP.
IF NOBODY CAN
HEAR YOU, HOW
WILL THEY

LISTEN??

WRITE YOURSELF A LETTER
NOW, THEN FOLD THE PAGE
& MARK A DATE TO OPEN
IT IN THE FUTURE.

KEEP ON
SCROLLING

NOTHING TO
SEE HERE

WRITE YOUR PROBLEMS
IN PENCIL NOW, THEN
ERASE THEM OVER TIME
UNTIL YOU'RE IN THE CLEAR.

NO MATTER WHERE YOU ARE,
GREAT THINGS ARE HAPPENING
AROUND YOU. SOMEONE'S KID
JUST SPOKE FOR THE FIRST
TIME. OLD FRIENDS ARE
REUNITING. IF THIS ISN'T
YOU TODAY, TOMORROW MIGHT
BE YOUR TURN FOR
    SOMETHING
        WONDERFUL.

WRITE A MESSAGE IN A BOTTLE
THEN CUT IT OUT & FLOAT IT AWAY
(DRAW MORE BOTTLES AS NEEDED)

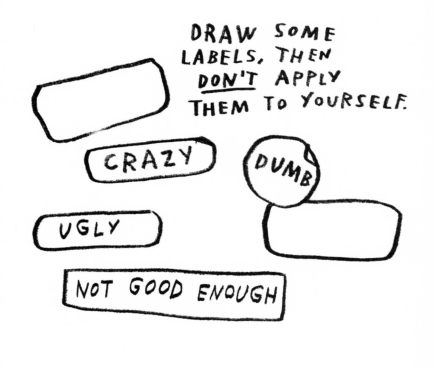

DRAW SOME
LABELS, THEN
DON'T APPLY
THEM TO YOURSELF.

CRAZY

DUMB

UGLY

NOT GOOD ENOUGH

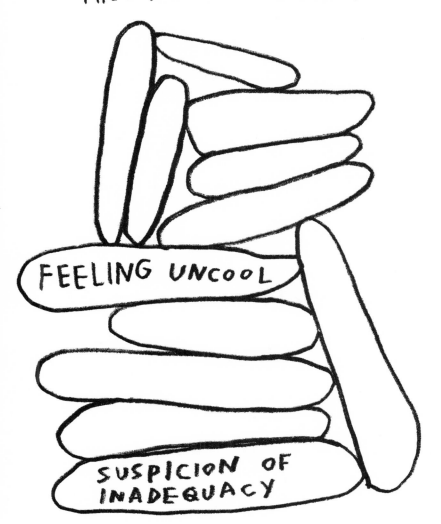

THERE ARE
SO MANY PEOPLE
IN THE WORLD & THEY
ALL HAVE BIG & SMALL
PROBLEMS & IT CAN
BE HELPFUL TO
REMEMBER THAT
LIFE IS JUST A
SERIES OF TASKS &
CHALLENGES &
MOMENTS &
FEELINGS FOR
EACH OF US.

MIDNIGHT THOUGHTS:

#PICKMEUPBOOK

IT CAN BE HARD
TO COMMUNICATE
SOMETIMES. TRY TO
REMEMBER THAT
EVERYONE IS
DIFFERENT, LIKE
SNOWFLAKES.

(IF SNOWFLAKES HAD
BRAINS THAT
PROCESSED THE WORLD
& THEIR EXPERIENCES
IN VASTLY DIFFERENT
WAYS.)

IT'S NICE THAT WE CAN BLAME THE MOON
FOR ALL OUR CRAZY EMOTIONS & BEHAVIOR!

CURRENT MOON: _____   ◯
MADE ME: _____

_____

_____

CURRENT MOON: _____   ◯
MADE ME: _____

_____

_____

CURRENT MOON: _____   ◯
MADE ME: _____

_____

_____

START HERE
& DRAW LOOPS
AROUND IN A
SINGLE,
SMOOTH
ACTION-

REPEAT
WHENEVER.

LOVE THIS PAGE,
THEN GIVE IT AWAY,
PIECE BY PIECE.

THINK ABOUT
WHAT YOU REALLY
WANT. TURN IT
OVER IN YOUR
MIND. HOLD THE
THOUGHT. VISUALIZE
IT FULLY.

NOW SNAP OUT
OF IT!! THIS IS
REAL LIFE.

SET ACTIONABLE
STEPS TOWARD
YOUR GOAL,
THEN ~~FUCKING~~
DO SOMETHING.

LETTING GO IS HARD.

PRACTICE BY PUTTING
THIS BOOK DOWN FOR
A BIT & MAYBE DOING
SOMETHING ELSE.

YOU MADE IT
TO THE LUCKIEST
PAGE IN THE BOOK!
THIS IS A GOOD SIGN.
HAVE A GREAT DAY!

MAKE A MESS NOW
& DIG YOURSELF OUT LATER:

OKAY BUT

THAT

SINKING

FEELING

MIGHT

HAVE

A

POINT

HAVE A PERSONAL BREAKTHROUGH

WRITE ABOUT YOUR PAST NOW,
THEN ADD MORE LATER. WHEN THE
PAGE IS FULL, TEAR THROUGH!

DRAW OVER A MISTAKE
TO MAKE SOMETHING NEW:

WHAT DOES <u>YOUR</u> MILK SHAKE BRING TO THE YARD?

☐ BOYS

☐ GIRLS

☐ GENDER IS A CONSTRUCT

☐ FRIENDS

☐ BRAIN FREEZE

☐ DIABETES

☐ #THIRST

☐ COPYRIGHT LAWYERS

☐ POSITIVE AFFIRMATION

☐ DROUGHT (NATURE'S THIRST)

☐ COWS/ HORSES

☐ TOURISTS

☐ TULIPS

☐ MORE MILK SHAKES

☐ THE BEATING OF HIS HIDEOUS HEART

SOMETIMES YOU JUST WANT
TO SCREAM & CRY BUT
YOU CAN'T. OTHER TIMES
YOU TOTALLY CAN!

FIND YOURSELF A SAFE,
PRIVATE SPACE TO
LET IT OUT. YOU ARE
AN AMAZING &

EMOTIONAL PERSON

WHO FEELS FEELINGS.

THIS CAN BE ANNOYING
SOMETIMES BUT IT'S
ALSO YOUR SECRET POWER.

KEEP BEING HUMAN.

PLANNING AHEAD IS ITS OWN REWARD.
WHAT'S YOUR PLAN FOR TODAY?

NOW _____

LATER _____

NEXT TIME _____

AGAIN _____

SOON _____

SOMETIME _____

ONCE MORE _____

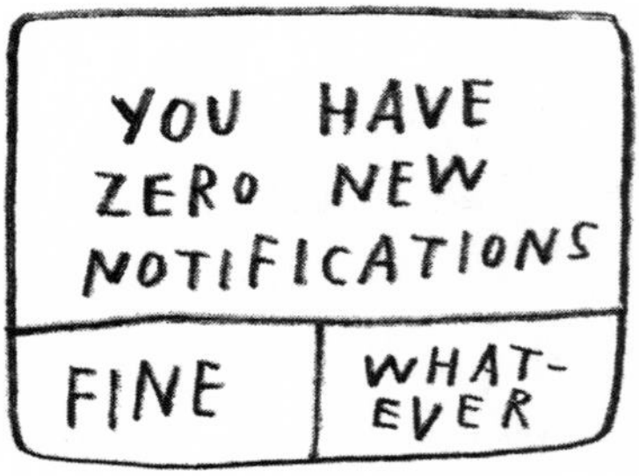
YOU HAVE ZERO NEW NOTIFICATIONS
FINE
WHAT-EVER

DRAW A MOLD, THEN PRACTICE NOT FITTING INTO IT.

DRAW A MOTIVATIONAL POSTER

NOW POST IT! #PICKMEUPBOOK

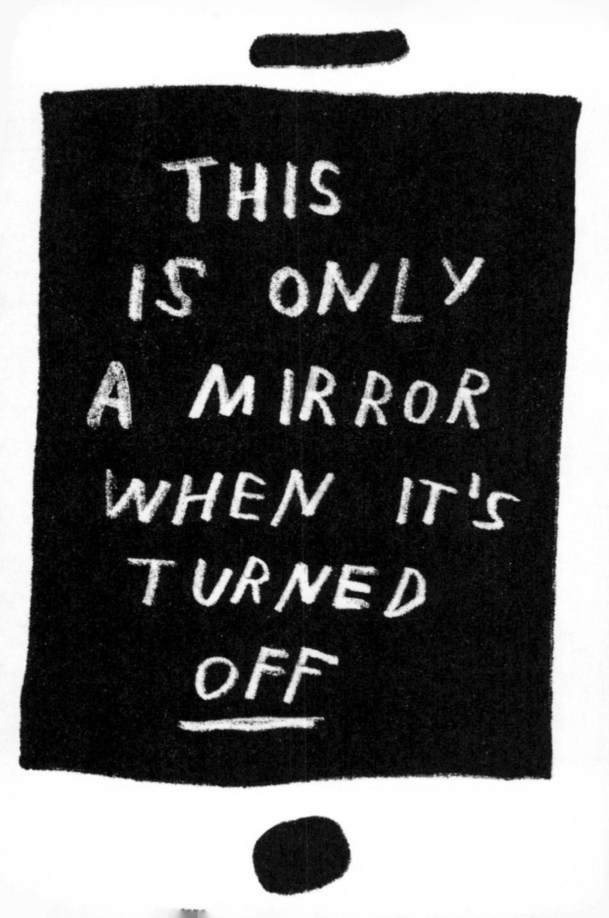
THIS IS ONLY A MIRROR WHEN IT'S TURNED OFF

WHAT'S YOUR FAVORITE SONG RIGHT NOW?

SONG: _____
ARTIST: _____
DATE: _____

SONG: _____
ARTIST: _____
DATE: _____

SONG: _____
ARTIST: _____
DATE: _____

SONG: _____
ARTIST: _____
DATE: _____

SONG: _____
ARTIST: _____
DATE: _____

SONG: _____
ARTIST: _____
DATE: _____

SONG: _____
ARTIST: _____
DATE: _____

SONG: _____
ARTIST: _____
DATE: _____

SONG: _____
ARTIST: _____
DATE: _____

SONG: _____
ARTIST: _____
DATE: _____

SONG: _____
ARTIST: _____
DATE: _____

SONG: _____
ARTIST: _____
DATE: _____

SHARE YOUR PLAYLIST WITH #PICKMEUPBOOK WHEN IT'S FULL

ROCK BEATS
SCISSORS,
BUT PAPER
WINS EVERY
TIME

GIVE SOMEONE YOUR NUMBER

CALL ME SOMETIME:

- - - - - - - - - - - - - - - - -

YOU'RE A TOTAL BABE:

- - - - - - - - - - - - - - -

TEXT ME AS LATE AS YOU WANT:

- - - - - - - - - - -

I'M SPEECHLESS NOW, CALL ME LATER:

- - - - - - - - - - - -

DID IT HURT WHEN YOU FELL FROM HEAVEN?

PROPOSED MANTRAS

- IT'S TOO BAD "COOL" IS A SOCIAL CONSTRUCT BECAUSE I AM PRETTY COOL

- ~~IF AT FIRST YOU DON'T SUCED~~

- PLEASE PASS THE CHOCOLATE
- I CAN DO ANYTHING IF I JUST PUT IT TO MY FOREHEAD & APPLY PRESSURE
- I AM DEFINITELY WORTH FOLLOWING ONLINE
- TO THINE SELFIE BE TRUE

WORK AROUND
THE OBSTACLES

POST THIS PAGE & TAG SOMEONE
FOR EACH BOX. COLOR IT IN FIRST!

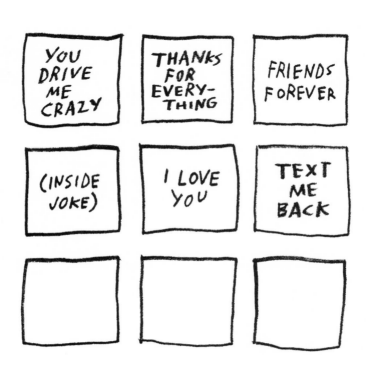

(FILL IN THE BLANKS!) #PICKMEUPBOOK

WHERE ARE YOU RIGHT NOW?

TIME _____

PLACE _____

TIME _____

PLACE _____

TIME _____

PLACE _____

TIME _____

PLACE _____

TIME _____

PLACE _____

TIME _____

PLACE _____

TIME _____

PLACE _____

TIME _____

PLACE _____

TIME _____

PLACE _____

TIME _____

PLACE _____

TIME _____

PLACE _____

TIME _____

PLACE _____

DO YOU EVER
FEEL LIKE
YOU HAVE
NO IDEA
WHAT YOU'RE
DOING???

SAME.
I THINK IT'S
NORMAL &
PROBABLY
OKAY.

RIGHT NOW I AM

_____

BUT I'D RATHER BE

_____

THIS TIME I'M

_____

BUT I'D RATHER BE

_____

UGH, I'M SO

_____

I WISH I WAS

_____

CURRENTLY

_____

CAN I PLEASE

_____

WHAT IS WRONG WITH YOU???

(SERIOUSLY, WRITE SOMETHING THAT'S NOT GREAT, THEN CROSS IT OUT NEXT TIME IF IT'S BETTER.)

EMOTIONAL BREAKDOWN

HOW DO YOU FEEL?

[ ]

WHY?   HOW LONG?   WHO KNOWS?

[ ]   [ ]   [ ]

WILL THIS LAST?

(YES)   (NO)

HOW WILL YOU   FORGET
HANDLE IT?   ABOUT IT!

[ ]

TODAY'S DATE: _____

NEVER
GIVING UP
IS HOW YOU
WIN.

SOMETHING YOU REALLY REALLY REALLY WANT RIGHT NOW:

NOW _____

LATER _____

NEXT TIME _____

AGAIN _____

SOON _____

SOMETIME _____

ONCE MORE _____

POWER's OUT!

BETTER RECHARGE

WHAT'S IN YOUR CUP?

GOAL TO ACCOMPLISH
BEFORE THE NEXT TIME YOU
RETURN TO THIS PAGE:

DID YOU DO IT? ☐ YES ☐ NO

REGULAR EGGS
CRACK & RUN
BUT NEST EGGS
APPRECIATE OVER TIME

LIFE IS TOO SHORT
TO PUT UP WITH
PEOPLE WHO DON'T
TREAT YOU WELL.

STICK UP FOR YOUR-
SELF. BE YOUR OWN
BIGGEST SUPPORTER.

YOU ARE WORTH IT.

YOU DESERVE THIS.

NEVER FORGET IT.

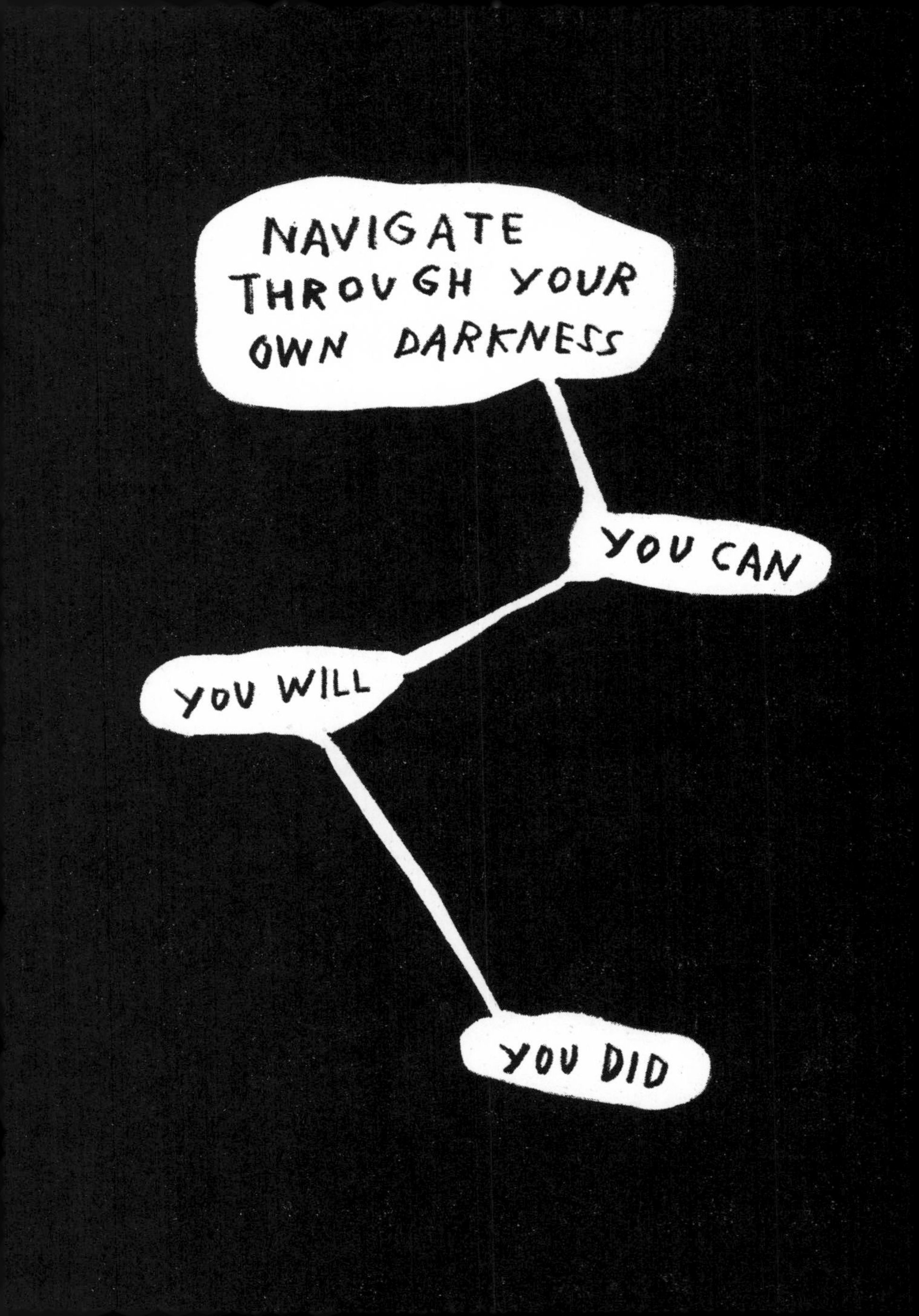
NAVIGATE THROUGH YOUR OWN DARKNESS
YOU CAN
YOU WILL
YOU DID

WRITE ONE NICE THING
ABOUT YOURSELF WHENEVER
YOU'RE ON THIS PAGE

_____   _____

_____   _____

_____   _____

_____   _____

_____   _____

_____   _____

_____   _____

_____   _____

_____   _____

_____   _____

WHAT'S THE NICEST THING
SOMEONE HAS SAID TO YOU
LATELY? ADD IT TO THE LIST!

NOW _____

LATER _____

NEXT TIME _____

AGAIN _____

SOON _____

SOMETIME _____

ONCE MORE _____

WRITE A TINY SECRET, THEN TEAR
IT OUT & HIDE IT. DO IT AGAIN & AGAIN
UNTIL THIS PAGE HAS DISAPPEARED.

I DON'T KNOW
WHERE YOU ARE
NOW BUT I AM
IN THE PAST,
THINKING ABOUT
YOUR FUTURE,
& I HOPE THAT
YOU ARE HAPPY.

WHAT DO
YOU THINK
WILL
HAPPEN
NEXT?

NEED SOME
ALONE TIME?

COVER YOURSELF
IN MIRRORS TO
APPEAR AS A
SHIMMERING
MIRAGE TO
PASSERSBY.

WRITE SOMETHING REALLY HONEST
THEN PRESS THE PAGE TO YOUR FACE
& FEEL THE WEIGHT OF YOUR TRUTH.

THINGS CAN'T JUST
GO BACK TO "HOW THEY WERE"
BECAUSE THERE IS NO BACK
& THERE NEVER CAN BE.
LIFE ONLY MOVES FORWARD.

STOP TRYING TO GO BACK
OR YOU WILL ALWAYS BE
DISAPPOINTED.
YOU WILL NEVER READ THIS
FOR THE FIRST TIME AGAIN.

FOLD THIS PAGE SHUT.
YOU CAN REVISIT IT,
BUT IT'S ALREADY
A MEMORY.

A NAGGING THOUGHT YOU CAN'T GET OUT OF YOUR HEAD TODAY

NOW _____

LATER _____

NEXT TIME _____

AGAIN _____

SOON _____

SOMETIME _____

ONCE MORE _____

WHO THE ~~FUCK~~ DO YOU
THINK YOU ARE??
ANSWER NOW, AGAIN
LATER, & TRACK YOUR
CHANGES.

BOOKS I'VE CLAIMED TO HAVE READ:

_____

_____

_____

_____

_____

_____

_____

LET'S JUST SIT HERE
& HOLD THIS PAGE
WITHOUT TALKING

WHAT ARE YOU GOOD AT?
WHAT MIGHT YOUR PURPOSE BE?
ADD ONE THING EACH VISIT
UNTIL THE PAGE IS USE-FULL!

_____   _____

_____   _____

_____   _____

_____   _____

_____   _____

_____   _____

_____   _____

_____   _____

TAPE A PHOTO OF YOURSELF
HERE & STARE YOURSELF DOWN

WRITE A SECRET THAT YOU SHOULDN'T TELL.
CHANGE ALL THE DETAILS. CROSS IT OUT.
DESTROY THE PAGE. OKAY, MAYBE JUST
DON'T DO ANYTHING TO BEGIN WITH.

OH GOOD!
HERE'S THAT SHORTCUT
YOU WERE LOOKING FOR

DRAW YOUR MIND
THEN LOSE IT:

DRAW A PIZZA.
ADD A TOPPING WHENEVER
YOU'RE HERE, THEN
    ORDER IT FOR REAL
        AFTER THE FIFTH TIME!

SOMETHING YOU DID THAT MIGHT
HAVE BEEN BAD BUT YOU DIDN'T
REALIZE IT AT THE TIME:

_____

_____

_____

_____

_____

_____

_____

SOMETHING YOU'D LIKE BUT WOULD NEVER BUY FOR YOURSELF:

TODAY

NEXT TIME

LATER

KEEP GOING

(NOW TREAT YOURSELF FROM THIS LIST!)

TEXT THIS PAGE
TO A FRIEND
WHENEVER YOU
LAND HERE.
MAKE IT EXTRA
COOL FIRST!

SLOWLY FILL THIS PAGE
WITH POSITIVE THOUGHTS,
THEN SHARE WHEN IT'S FULL

_____   _____

_____   _____

_____   _____

_____   _____

_____   _____

_____   _____

_____   _____

_____   _____

_____   _____

_____   _____

📷 #PICKMEUPBOOK

SOMETHING I NEED TO REMEMBER:

DRAW YOURSELF
A BLANK REALITY
CHECK FOR LATER.

WRITE A SECRET MOTIVATION
ON THE BOTTOM OF YOUR
SHOE & THEN HIT THE
GROUND RUNNING!

HOW TO THROW AN EFFECTIVE TANTRUM

- LOSE YOUR COOL IMMEDIATELY TO ENSURE NOBODY WANTS TO COME NEAR YOU.

- IF SOMEONE DOES TRY TO HELP, SHOUT "YOU DON'T UNDERSTAND!" NOBODY ELSE HAS EVER HAD A BAD DAY BEFORE.

- BREAK SOMETHING YOU OWN. THAT WAY YOU STILL SUFFER EVEN WHEN YOU HAVE CALMED DOWN.

- RANT ONLINE, BECAUSE THERE'S NOTHING QUITE AS SATISFYING AS SELF—SABOTAGE!

GET A SONG
OUT OF YOUR HEAD
BY PUTTING IT HERE:

ARTIST:

SONG:

SAMPLE LYRIC:

ARTIST:

SONG:

SAMPLE LYRIC:

ARTIST:

SONG:

SAMPLE LYRIC:

ARTIST:

SONG:

SAMPLE LYRIC:

CHARGE UP THE PAGE
UNTIL IT'S FULL:

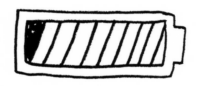

GREAT! YOU HAVE THE
POWER TO DO ANYTHING!

WHAT CAN YOU MAKE
FROM (ALMOST) NOTHING?

ADD SOMETHING NEW NOW
& AGAIN LATER!

UPDATE YOUR STATUS:

NOW

LATER

AGAIN

ONCE MORE

LOSE YOUR TRAIN OF THOUGHT
BY STARTING SOMETHING HERE
& CONTINUING ON ANOTHER PAGE.

WRITE A LIST OF THINGS
THAT ARE BAD NOW, THEN
CROSS THEM OFF AS
THEY BECOME IRRELEVANT

_____   _____

_____   _____

_____   _____

_____   _____

_____   _____

_____   _____

_____   _____

_____   _____

_____   _____

_____   _____

GIVE THESE AWAY UNTIL
YOU HAVE ZERO Fs TO GIVE!

OR GIVE THEM ONLINE #PICKMEUPBOOK

A REALLY STRONG,
POSITIVE FEELING:

NOW _____

LATER _____

NEXT TIME _____

AGAIN _____

SOON _____

SOMETIME _____

ONCE MORE _____

COMMEMORATE THE SMALL MOMENTS
WITH SOME QUICK LITTLE DRAWINGS:

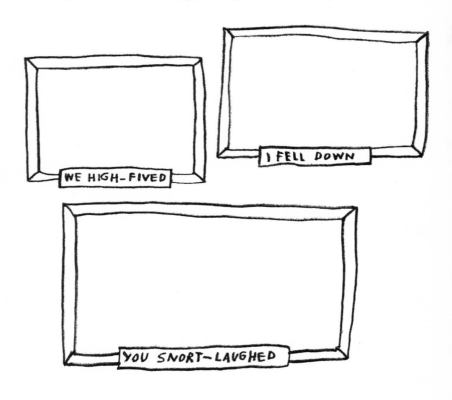

WE HIGH-FIVED

I FELL DOWN

YOU SNORT-LAUGHED

SHARE THESE MEMORIES #PICKMEUPBOOK

TRY TO DRAW SOMETHING
DIFFICULT, THEN GIVE UP
UNTIL NEXT TIME:

FILL THIS SPACE
SO YOU'RE NEVER
   ALONE:

IF THE DOOR
ISN'T LOCKED,
JUST OPEN IT AGAIN!

THE STUPIDEST THING YOU'VE DONE RECENTLY:

NOW _____

LATER _____

NEXT TIME _____

AGAIN _____

SOON _____

SOMETIME _____

ONCE MORE _____

(IT'S OKAY, WE'RE ALL JUST KIND OF BUMBLING IDIOTS)

TRY DRAWING SOMETHING NEW:

A HORSE:

BUNCH OF BANANAS:

MOMENT OF TRUTH:

MOUNTAIN TOP:

YOUR OWN NOSE:

OUTER SPACE:

EVERYONE HAS A SOUL MATE,
PROBABLY? DRAW THINGS
THAT COME IN PAIRS:

WHEN YOU LOOK UP
AT THE SKY, WHO ARE
YOU THINKING OF?

WHAT'S AROUND YOU?
DRAW ONE NEARBY THING NOW
& AGAIN LATER UNTIL YOU'RE
COMPLETELY SURROUNDED!

DRAW YOUR OWN SUPPORT SYSTEM

DRAW A SOUVENIR FROM A MOMENT OR FEELING:

DISGUISE YOUR TERROR BY
WRAPPING IT IN OTHER
                    EMOTIONS:

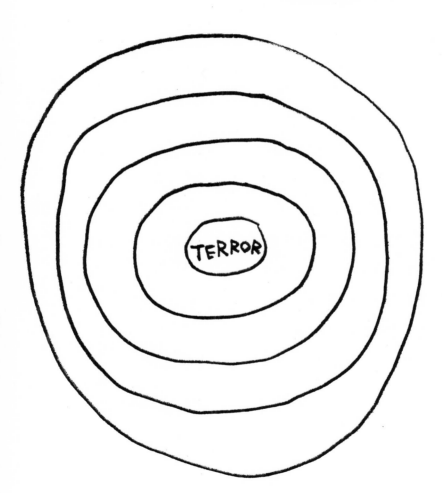

WHAT HAVE YOU ALREADY DONE?

- ☐ ACED A TEST
- ☐ BEEN MARRIED
- ☐ HAD BREAKFAST
- ☐ 100 LIKES
- ☐ BRUSHED HAIR
- ☐ CELEB SIGHTING
- ☐ BROKEN BONE
- ☐ TRUE LOVE
- ☐ PET A DOLPHIN
- ☐ PLANT A TREE
- ☐ DANCE LIKE NOBODY'S WATCHING

- ☐ CRIED ALL NIGHT
- ☐ SWIM IN AN OCEAN
- ☐ DRINK 8 CUPS OF WATER
- ☐ ROLL DOWN A HILL
- ☐ LEARN ANOTHER LANGUAGE
- ☐ GET A TATTOO
- ☐ HAVE THE LAST LAUGH
- ☐ DANCE LIKE SOMEBODY IS WATCHING

GIVE YOURSELF A TIP:

DRAW THE VEGETABLES
YOU DON'T LIKE, THEN
CROSS THEM OUT AS
YOU GET OVER IT.
(YOU BIG BABY)

THIS HAPPENED: _____

_____

BUT IT WAS OKAY BECAUSE: _____

_____

THEN THIS: _____

_____

AND IT WAS FINE BECAUSE: _____

_____

& THEN: _____

_____

BUT: _____

_____

WHAT ARE SOME THINGS
YOU CAN CONTROL?
START A LIST NOW
& ADD MORE LATER.

_____   _____

_____   _____

_____   _____

_____   _____

_____   _____

_____   _____

_____   _____

_____   _____

_____   _____

_____   _____

WRITE A THANK-YOU NOTE
TO SOMEONE YOU WON'T
SEE AGAIN. PUT IT INTO THE
UNIVERSE WITH #PICKMEUPBOOK!

THE "WORST" THING ON YOUR CURRENT TO-DO LIST

NOW _____

LATER _____

NEXT TIME _____

AGAIN _____

SOON _____

SOMETIME _____

ONCE MORE _____

DRAW THE VIEW FROM YOUR WINDOW:

RIGHT NOW

KINDA SOON

ANOTHER TIME

MUCH LATER

FILL THE PAGE WITH WAVES
SLOWLY OVER TIME & STARE
AT THEM TO FEEL CALM LATER.

WAVES ALWAYS BREAK BUT
THEY NEVER STOP COMING.

WHAT DO YOU DO WHEN
NOTHING MAKES SENSE??
WHAT OR WHO CAN HELP?

THE ANSWER

COME BACK IF YOU FORGET

DRAW A CURRENT EMOTION:

STRESSED

THE BEST PART OF YOUR DAY

NOW _____

LATER _____

NEXT TIME _____

AGAIN _____

SOON _____

SOMETIME _____

ONCE MORE _____

ANYTHING ✦
CAN BE ✦
SPECIAL IF ✦
YOU CHERISH IT.

✦ WHAT DO
    YOU LOVE?

EMOTIONAL BREAKDOWN

HOW DO YOU FEEL?

[ ]

WHY?

[ ]

HOW LONG?

[ ]

WHO KNOWS?

[ ]

WILL THIS LAST?

(YES)

(NO)

HOW WILL YOU HANDLE IT?

FORGET ABOUT IT!

[ ]

TODAY'S DATE: _____

THE | VERY TOP | OF THIS | WHOLE PAGE

SLOWLY WORK | YOUR WAY | UP | TO

THINGS I'M DEFINITELY
GOING TO FORGET, BUT
DON'T WANT TO:

_____

_____

_____

_____

_____

_____

_____

FILL IN YOUR FUTURE!

PREDICTION

THIS CAN
BE A
MEETING
PLACE

SEE YOU AGAIN SOON

THANK YOU:

- PENCILS

- COFFEE

- MITCHELL, JEREMY, TUESDAY, JESSE, HALLIE & SARAH

- TERROR

- A CUTE DOG I SAW

- THE INTERNET

- BRAZIL!!!!!!!

- MARIAN (EDITOR) MONIKA (AGENT) MYSELF (LOL)

FOLLOW @ADAMJK
OR VISIT ADAMJK.COM

Photo by David Brookton

Adam J. Kurtz is a Brooklyn-based artist and author whose first book, *1 Page at a Time*, has been translated into fifteen languages.

His "very personal" personal work has been featured in *Fast Company*, *Paper*, *Nylon*, *BuzzFeed*, *HOW*, *Refinery29*, *Design*Sponge* and elsewhere. He has collaborated with brands like Tumblr, Urban Outfitters, Fishs Eddy, Strand Bookstore and Brooklyn Public Library, and worked for clients including the *New York Times*, Pepsi and Adobe.